S0-EIL-080

# NATURAL DISASTERS

# Droughts

by Rebecca Pettiford

BLASTOFF!
3
READERS

BELLWETHER MEDIA • MINNEAPOLIS, MN

Note to Librarians, Teachers, and Parents:

**Blastoff! Readers** are carefully developed by literacy experts and combine standards-based content with developmentally appropriate text.

**Level 1** provides the most support through repetition of high-frequency words, light text, predictable sentence patterns, and strong visual support.

**Level 2** offers early readers a bit more challenge through varied simple sentences, increased text load, and less repetition of high-frequency words.

**Level 3** advances early-fluent readers toward fluency through increased text and concept load, less reliance on visuals, longer sentences, and more literary language.

**Level 4** builds reading stamina by providing more text per page, increased use of punctuation, greater variation in sentence patterns, and increasingly challenging vocabulary.

**Level 5** encourages children to move from "learning to read" to "reading to learn" by providing even more text, varied writing styles, and less familiar topics.

Whichever book is right for your reader, Blastoff! Readers are the perfect books to build confidence and encourage a love of reading that will last a lifetime!

This edition first published in 2020 by Bellwether Media, Inc.

No part of this publication may be reproduced in whole or in part without written permission of the publisher. For information regarding permission, write to Bellwether Media, Inc., Attention: Permissions Department, 6012 Blue Circle Drive, Minnetonka, MN 55343.

Library of Congress Cataloging-in-Publication Data

Names: Pettiford, Rebecca, author.
Title: Droughts / Rebecca Pettiford.
Description: Minneapolis : Bellwether Media, [2020] | Series: Blastoff readers! Natural disasters | Includes bibliographical references and index. | Audience: Ages 5-8. | Audience: Grades 2-3. | Summary: "Simple text and full-color photography introduce beginning readers to droughts. Developed by literacy experts for students in kindergarten through third grade"-- Provided by publisher.
Identifiers: LCCN 2019028733 (print) | LCCN 2019028734 (ebook) | ISBN 9781644871508 (library binding) | ISBN 9781618918260 (ebook)
Subjects: LCSH: Droughts--Juvenile literature. | Natural disasters--Juvenile literature.
Classification: LCC QC929.25 .P48 2020 (print) | LCC QC929.25 (ebook) | DDC 551.57/73--dc23
LC record available at https://lccn.loc.gov/2019028733
LC ebook record available at https://lccn.loc.gov/2019028734

Text copyright © 2020 by Bellwether Media, Inc. BLASTOFF! READERS and associated logos are trademarks and/or registered trademarks of Bellwether Media, Inc.

Editor: Rebecca Sabelko      Designer: Josh Brink

Printed in the United States of America, North Mankato, MN

# Table of Contents

# What Are Droughts?

Droughts are long periods with little or no rain. They happen slowly over time.

They can cause a lot of damage. But droughts are hard to **predict**.

## Major Droughts Since 2000

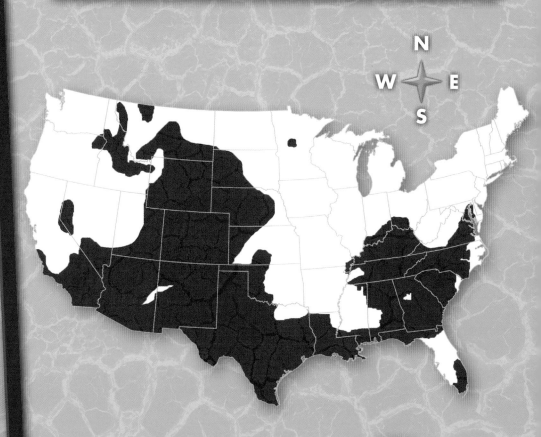

N
W E
S

major drought areas =

# How Do Droughts Form?

Droughts form when there is not enough **precipitation**. The amount of water that falls is caused by **weather patterns**.

Water **evaporates** and forms clouds. Winds carry the clouds. These winds are called the **jet stream**.

Sometimes weather patterns can block the jet stream. This can cause the weather in an area to change.

## How Droughts Form

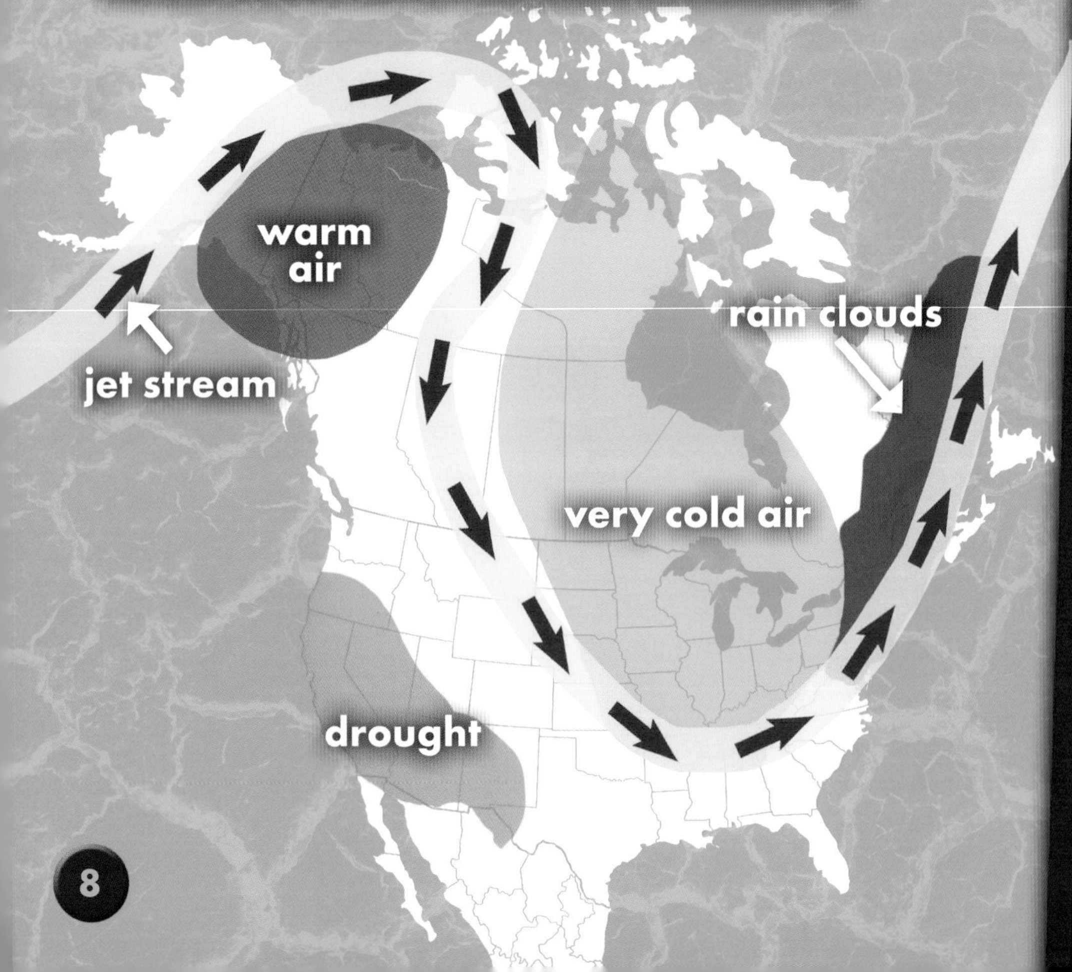

warm
air

jet stream

rain clouds

very cold air

drought

Droughts form when
rain clouds are blocked.
Little to no rain falls.

**Climate change** causes droughts, too. **Moisture** evaporates from the ground when **temperatures** rise.

Moisture also evaporates from lakes and rivers. This can lead to droughts!

# Drought Damage

Droughts cause many problems. Food cannot grow. This leads to **famine**. People may be forced to move.

Animals may struggle to survive. **Ecosystems** change as animals move and different types of plants grow.

# Drought Index

| Drought Level | State of Soil |
|---|---|
| -4.0 or less: | • extremely dry |
| -3.0 to -3.9: | • severely dry |
| -2.0 to -2.9: | • unusually dry |
| -1.9 to +1.9: | • near normal |
| +2.0 to +2.9: | • unusually wet |
| +3.0 to +3.9: | • very wet |
| +4.0 and above: | • extremely wet |

clearing trees

People often make droughts worse. They use too much water. They clear trees. This puts more harmful gases into the air.

These practices speed up climate change. They make droughts last much longer!

overusing water

# Predicting Disaster

It is hard to know when droughts will happen. They often have more than one cause.

The **U.S. Drought Monitor** can help. It allows people to predict how bad droughts will be.

# Drought Profile

**Name:** 1988-1989 North American Drought

**Dates:** 1988-1989, 1990 in some areas

**Location:** much of the United States and parts of Canada

**Damage to Property:** 683,000 acres (2,764 square kilometers) of Yellowstone National Park affected by wildfires

**Damage to People:** up to 10,000 lives lost

There are ways to plan for a drought. Begin saving water today!

Do not pour clean water down the sink. Use it to water plants or clean the house.

Turn the water off when it is not being used. Take short showers instead of baths.

These practices can make a big difference during a drought!

# Glossary

**climate change**—a human-caused process in which Earth's average weather changes over a long period of time

**ecosystems**—groups of living and nonliving things that make up environments and affect each other

**evaporates**—changes from a liquid to a gas

**famine**—a shortage of food

**jet stream**—the high-speed winds high above the earth's surface

**moisture**—water or other liquid

**precipitation**—the amount of water that falls to the earth as hail, mist, rain, sleet, or snow

**predict**—to use information to guess what may happen

**temperatures**—how cold or hot things are

**U.S. Drought Monitor**—a map that shows where droughts are located in the United States

**weather patterns**—weather conditions that stay the same for a period of time in one area

# To Learn More

## AT THE LIBRARY

Herman, Gail. *What Is Climate Change?* New York, N.Y.: Penguin Workshop, 2018.

Olien, Rebecca. *Saving Water*. North Mankato, Minn.: Capstone Press, 2016.

Stewart, Melissa. *Droughts*. New York, N.Y.: Harper, 2017.

## ON THE WEB

# FACTSURFER

Factsurfer.com gives you a safe, fun way to find more information.

1. Go to www.factsurfer.com.

2. Enter "droughts" into the search box and click 🔍

3. Select your book cover to see a list of related web sites.

# Index

The images in this book are reproduced through the courtesy of: Ryan Morgan, front cover (tree); Andrei Bortnikau, front cover (background); 24Novembers, front cover (ground), p. 4; Thinnapob Proongsak, pp. 2-3; HelloRF Zcool, p. 6; MICHELANGELOBOY, p. 7; Suzanne Tucker, p. 9; bibiphoto, p. 10; Quintanilla, p. 11; SMMick, p. 12; Wildeside, p. 13; Rich Carey, p. 14; Ekaterina_Molchanova, p. 15; Rick Bowmer/ AP Images, p. 16; Krisztian Juhasz, p. 17; Graphic.mooi, p. 18; Lucian Coman p. 19; wavebreakmedia, p. 20; Sawat Banyenngam, p. 21.